The Deal Is Real
GODS Pension Plan for Man

GODS presence in a deal signifies truth, commitment, and ever-lasting faith. It is through such divine intervention that one can truly understand the depth of promises made and kept. Only then does the essence of the deal become real.

Johnnie R. Capers

For permission requests, write to the author, addressed to:

Johnnie R. Capers

Email Address

jonrobcapers@yahoo.com

Dedication

First, Foremost, I Dedicate this book to GOD In JESUS Christ for my life with all its strife, tears, and Beautiful Days of Happiness with family, friends, and every woman I've loved, cherished, willfully surrendered to in shared Spirit of GOD'S Divine Love. My Love for, and to, you are Forever.

Johnnie Robert Capers

Acknowledgement

LORD GOD, Dear Father, Thank You for Blessing me with Love, Strength, Stamina, Understanding, and Knowledge required to write this book. I Thank all those who slandered, abandoned, deserted me, wallowing in my unrequited love for them. No ill feelings are permitted here. I LOVE AND FORGIVE EVERYONE OF YOU.

We Are All Children of GOD assigned to, given provision to achieve, our GOD worshipping, GOD praising, GOD praying, GOD trusting roles of assignment in GODS Master Plan for Man replete with Real Deal Pension Plan for Man.

Table of Contents

Forward

For all pondering the reality of GODS Existence, *"The Deal is Real, GODS Pension Plan for Man"* is clear in delivery from Egypt[1] back to The Garden of Eden renewing our relationship with, and divine thought about, the awesome power of our Creator. Forsaking all else a mustard seed-sized faith seeking for GOD embraces heart and mind in want of, demanding to know, all there is about the true goodness of GOD. A process that removes focus on carnal, seen things, to focus on things unseen in nature that transcend time and space fueling the transformation of one's mind with the ability to communicate with powerful, unseen, life-sustaining forces that are the servants of GOD. All of GOD'S Creations Praise and Serve GOD cheerfully under the Stewardship of man. GOD Assigns Angels to keep watch over you and me from cradle to grave but for our satanic blinded self-willed sinful rebellion to destruction grieving GOD in rejection. Yet, according to His hierarchy, GOD still reserves residence in Heaven for all of us.

---

[1] Egypt is a state of mind and being mentally oppressive and immobilizing one to wilful embrace of self-imposed bondage due to lack of knowledge of The Reciprocal Nature Of GOD.

Preface

Hurt nor harm to anyone, wishing loving peace to everyone, in this work please permit Egypt to be "a state of mind and being" not favorable to reciprocation. With that said, may blessings be upon you all.

On any given day, many of us seek deliverance from Egypt back to our prearranged position in The Garden of Eden as a divine renewal of our thought process. A divine renewing from focusing on carnal things to focusing on unseen spiritual forces transforming our minds and keeping them in union with the Creator, Sustainer, of all life and creation. We are born into a "Work of our hand's world" overseen by performance accolades, rewarding pay bonuses, a reinforced process of self-dependent life-changing incentives designed for conformity to dependence on what was created, rather than transforming into likeness and image of our Creator who has bequeathed us everything as faithful heirs to His Promises.

Reading the Bible regularly, I've often reminisced about the years of my life making comparisons to the wisdom of the Holy Scripture I failed to heed; it dawned on me that I was blocking the pathway to everything I ever wanted in life. Like a windowless room being flooded with light, the reality of GOD's Promises illuminated my mind. All that I was searching for was already mine if I would only live up to my end of "The LORD is my Shephard, I shall not want" Provision offered to me – and all other human beings, free of charge by GOD, the Creator. The Deal is Real; GOD's Pension Plan for Man truly exists if we humbly stand tall in obedient faith, belief, and genuine trust in GOD, Our Creator, Miracle Worker, and Owner of Eternity.

"The Real Deal Relationship"

As far back as I can remember, even as early as age 4, everyone I knew or heard of sought, hoped, and prayed for something or someone that would transform their life into all they ever dreamed their life would be. Every one of us was seeking a "Real Deal Relationship" that would enable us to achieve our heart's ultimate desires in life. The "Real Deal Relationship" that makes your dreams come true connoted equity to everyone who dared to dream but lacked a source of achievement. Yet, it seemed to me that we all embraced a mindset that cast doubt on GOD's Ability to fulfill our heart's desire, dream come true, Real Deal. The adage "GOD helps those who help themselves" echoed in my ears for years as I labored under self-dependence lacking the belief and trust in GOD required to truly prosper. So, taking the adage "GOD helps those who help themselves" to heart, I've focused virtually all my adult life on "Self-dependence[2]" to make my life what I want it to be. Blinded by self-dependence, I failed to perceive my enslavement to desires, dreams, self-serving traditions, and ceremonies conjured up in my mind by man-induced illusions that define what my life should be albeit in defiance of GOD's Guarantee to make my every dream come true if I stayed focused on Him.

---

[2] Self-dependance is a human-mindset that only trusts and considers what one's self can do and achieve giving no consideration to GOD'S Promises nor GOD'S Ability as Creator of Everything.

Nonetheless, my physical well-being along with my psychological, social, and spiritual growth was stunted by my focus on self-serving "I'm-ma-do"[3] worldly endeavors cherishing worthless things. It never entered my mind to give serious thought to the Creator's instructions for a full-potential life for all human beings who stayed focused on HIM. A full-potential life positively affects all other creations while relishing GOD's, The Creator's Real Deal Relationship.

It all happened one day as I sat reading the Bible, it dawned on me that the Real Deal I was searching for was already mine if I would only live up to my end of the Real Deal Provision offered to me, and all other human beings, free of charge by GOD, the Creator of everything. However, I also realized that the problem with honoring the Creator's Real Deal Provision was that it displaced me as the center of my universe prompting me to choose my perceived truth over GOD's, The Creator's Everlasting Truth. Everlasting Truth that I now know fulfills the Real Deal Provisions that so many human beings are searching for. The Deal Is Real, GOD'S Pension Plan for Man exists having been set in place when GOD created man. We share ownership of everything with our Creator when we humbly stand tall in obedient faith, belief, and genuine trust in GOD, our Creator as heirs to the covenant revelation of Romans 5:19 *"For as by one man's disobedience many were made sinners, so also by one Man's obedience many will be made righteous."*

---

[3] I'm-ma-do is a defiant spirit of self-righteousness that asserts, I'm going to show you what I can and will do regarding a matter or concerning a given situation.

I.   God Created All to Work Together

There are millions, approximately 10 billion stars positioned throughout the universe sharing characteristics that classify them as stars. Stars are constantly being born in the universe as human beings are constantly being born on earth. Stars fall from the sky, the universe, just as human beings on earth pass away, physically die, reverting into dust from whence all flesh came. However, stars and human beings alike radiate life force energy within the dust they are made of before being recycled back into the dust from whence all came. The life force energy that radiates within each human being be it good, bad, or indifferent, is manifested to all other human beings by the life legacy each human being leaves behind. Just as a shooting star to some eyes, or a falling star to other eyes, streaks through the sky marveling the minds of human beings who observe its trajectory. In like fashion, the life legacy a human being leaves behind marvels the minds of human beings that live on to usher those deceased on in spiritual transformation. The life legacy left behind by some human beings marvels at the minds of living human beings in a pleasant manner making them feel that humanity has truly suffered a loss due to their passing on. Likewise, the life legacy left behind by some human beings is looked upon by living human beings with disdain and a feeling that the world is a better place now that the individual has passed on. Nonetheless, GOD, The Creator, will tally the Life Legacy Ledger written by each of us via our life endeavors in the Land of the Living when our flesh returns to the dust from which GOD, the Creator, lent it to us. Ultimately, all that we perform in life, in the darkness of earth will be revealed, made transparent for all to see, in GOD's, the Creator's Universal Light of Righteousness foretold in Matthew 7:21-23:

"Not everyone who says to Me, 'Lord, Lord,' shall enter the kingdom of heaven, but he who does the will of My Father in heaven. Many will say to Me in that day, 'Lord, Lord, have we not prophesied in Your name, cast out demons in Your name, and done many wonders in Your name?' And then I will declare to them, 'I never knew you; depart from Me, you who practice lawlessness!"

II. The Great Job, Loving Spouse, Wealth Creation Illusion.

The companionship of GOD sets free enslaved captives in every walk of life. There's not a captive that GOD, the Creator, cannot set free, but for our free will having been created in the image and likeness of GOD, the Creator. The human problem is we have been lulled into embracing, and loving for, "Self-dependence" in defiance of "GOD Dependence" which is the foundation of GOD's Real Deal Provision that is freely offered to all human beings in the salvation of JESUS CHRIST, Isa, Yeshua, GOD Himself:

"The Lord will establish you as a holy people to Himself, just as He has sworn to you if you keep the commandments of the Lord your God and walk in His ways. Then all peoples of the earth shall see that you are called by the name of the Lord, and they shall be afraid of you." (Deuteronomy 28:9-10)

And John 15:12-19; made manifest for you to read openly, freely, here in The Deal Is Real; GOD's Pension Plan for Man:

"This is My commandment, that you love one another as I have loved you. Greater love has no one than this than to lay down one's life for his friends. You are My friends if you do whatever I command you. No longer do I call you servants, for a servant does not know what his master is doing; but I have called you friends, for all things that I heard from My Father I have made known to you. You did not choose Me, but I chose you and appointed you that you should go and bear fruit and that your fruit should remain, that whatever you ask the Father in My name He may give you. These things I command you, that you love one another. If the world hates you, you know that it hated Me before it hated you. If you were of the world, the world would love its own. Yet because you are not of the world, but I chose you out of the world, therefore the world hates you." (John 15:12 -19)

However, we become hypnotized by worldly illusions, sights, things, sounds, and people that collectively forge a mindset in us that alienates us from and frowns upon, GOD-dependence. We forget that GOD's Word guarantees us victory in all things when we are focused on and strive for GOD-dependence. When we have done our best in endeavors pleasing to GOD, we will be fruitful, in good health, with unceasing prosperity that makes our very worst day nothing more than victory rehearsal for battles yet unseen or unknown. However, we fail GOD and fall short of peacefulness in our endeavors marooned in our destructive "I'm-ma-do" spirit of self-dependence rather than leaning on, inpraise-filled prayer, the GOD-dependent Spirit of Victory that conquers all opposition to The Goodness GOD Has for us in the Land of the Living. Embracing GOD-dependence is the revival of days of old when the Spirit of GOD went before us Victoriously Providing our every need. GOD's Love for us, human beings, is the same Love GOD has for JESUS CHRIST made evident by GOD accepting our rejection of GOD for a human king to rule over us. What we need is a revival of the days of old. A new beginning of obedience to GOD that is made manifest to all by the evolution of our character through actions and deeds compelled by the Holy Spirit taking residence in us. When the Holy Spirit takes residence in us, we no longer see merit nor gain in deeds, actions, or endeavors that alienate us from GOD's Blessings and Holy Grace. GOD makes it clear to all that our well-being is His Focus in 2 Chronicles 7:14:

"If My people, which are called by My name, shall humble themselves, and pray, and seek My face, and turn from their wicked ways; then will I hear from heaven, and will forgive their sin, and will heal their land."

Lord GOD compelled this Holy Scripture, all Holy Scripture, for our well-being for all eternity. There is no declaration of poverty being our Holy Portion nor our portion in any way but for our free will. No, the Word of GOD guarantees prosperity to all who work and labor to the Glory of GOD spoken in Colossians 3:23-24:

"Whatever you do, work heartily, as for the Lord and not for men, knowing that from the Lord you will receive the inheritance as your reward. You are serving the Lord Christ."

Thus, there is no declaration from GOD demanding we break our backs or minds in work for someone else other than ourselves. Without work we will not eat is agreed upon by most people. GOD will bless all work of our hands that is pleasing to GOD. We must concentrate our efforts on doing any work that is morally pleasing to GOD. Daily we must get up and do something that GOD can bless us through. Unceasing worship, praise, prayer, and obedience to

GOD in JESUS CHRIST's, Yeshua's, Holy Name, Holy Blood, and Holy Word are the work GOD created us for. However, our embrace of the satanic curse of "I'm-ma-do" self-dependence alienates us from GOD's Miracles, Blessing, and Loving smile. We must return in Spirit of Love laboring to Bless Lord GOD in actions and deeds spoken of by Isaiah:

"Is not this the kind of fasting I have chosen: to loose the chains of injustice and untie the cords of the yoke, to set the oppressed free and break every yoke? Is it not to share your food with the hungry and to provide the poor wanderer with shelter, when you see the naked to clothe him, and not to turn away from your own flesh and blood? Then your light will break forth like the dawn, and your healing will quickly appear; then your righteousness will go before you, and the glory of the Lord will be your rear guard. Then you will call, and the Lord will answer; you will cry for help, and He will say: Here am I." (Isaiah 58:6-9)

Knowing from seeing the Word of GOD with our own eyes with total belief that GOD doesn't lie, our reality should find us walking in and enacting Psalm 55:22:

"Cast thy burden upon the LORD, and he shall sustain thee: he shall never suffer the righteous to be moved." (Psalm 55:22)

Thus, there is no room for misunderstanding the Words of GOD. Everything belongs to GOD. *"It all belongs to GOD. As do you and I,"* Those words are hard for many of us to fully comprehend and earnestly believe as we long for GOD's Loving kindness seeking the Kingdom of GOD in the land of the living as spoken in the Lord's Prayer by JESUS CHRIST, Yeshua, Isa:

"Thine will be done on earth as it is in Heaven, Give us this day our daily bread; and forgive us our trespasses as we forgive those who trespass against us..."

GOD Gives each one of us daily forgiveness and daily bread to sustain us against the evil that we blindly adore and betray GOD for time and again. Many a day of our lives we completely forget Salvation and Prosperity belong to GOD, and to GOD alone! In our forgetfulness, we become fixated on our 'By the work my hands and might of my mind' great job, loving wife, financial security syndrome that isolates us from the Goodness of GOD-dependence. Our focus stays on self-dependence via the work of our hands and the might of our minds. So, far removed from our consciousness are remembrances of the dream-fulfilling lovingkindness of GOD-dependence. We toil under influence of the self-righteous spirit of Caine, all the while, requesting GOD bless the work of our hands as spoken of in Deuteronomy 28:12:

"The Lord will open the heavens, the storehouse of His bounty, to send rain on your land in season and to bless all the work of your hands. You will lend to many nations but will borrow from none." (Deuteronomy 28:12)

We petition GOD to bless the work of our hands. The work of our hands with minds that do what...?

"So you shall not turn aside from any of the words which I command you thisday, to the right or the left, to go after other gods to serve them." (Deut. 28:14)

Makes quite clear that what our hearts and our minds are stayed on will have a profound effect on the work of our hands in our claim of GOD's Blessings while avoiding idolatry against GOD in the form of a "I'm-ma-do" spirit of self-dependence.

The idolatry of self-dependence cloaks itself in the arrogance of the "I'm-ma-do" spirit that elevates oneself as the center of the universe. Such idolatry compels manipulation of everything and everybody to the achievement of one's wants, desires, and self-serving aggrandizement in life with little thought for GOD as the provider. The time we reserve for GOD in our lives becomes virtually nonexistent when our focus is on self-dependency. Blinded like Esau, or even arrogant Nimrod, there is little consideration of GOD as the true source of our goodness when our minds are focused on and under control of the spirit of "I'm-ma-do" self-dependence. Close examination of the words of Psalm 103 reveals the benefits, GOD Reserved Benefits, for all who humble themselves to the Victorious Spirit of GOD-dependence forsaking "I'm-ma-do" spiritual blindness of self-dependence.

PSALM 103

"Bless the Lord, O my soul: and all that is within me, bless his holy name. Bless the Lord, O my soul, and forget not all his benefits: Who forgiveth all thine iniquities; who healeth all thy diseases; Who redeemeth thy life from destruction; who crowneth thee with lovingkindness and tender mercies; Who satisfieth thy mouth with good things; so that thy youth is renewed like the eagle's. The Lord executeth righteousness and judgment for all that are oppressed. He made known his ways unto Moses, his acts unto the children of Israel. The Lord is merciful and gracious, slow to anger,

and plenteous in mercy. He will not always strive with us, neither will he keep his anger forever. He hath not dealt with us after our sins; nor rewarded us according to our iniquities. For as the heaven is high above the earth, so great is his mercy toward them that fear him. As far as the east is from the west, so far hath he removed our transgressions from us. Like as a father pitieth his children, so the Lord pitieth them that fear him. For he knoweth our frame; he remembereth that we are dust. As for man, his days are as grass: as a flower of the field, so he flourisheth. For the wind passeth over it, and it is gone; and the place thereof shall know it no more. But the mercy of the Lord is from everlasting to everlasting upon them that fear him, and his righteousness unto children's children; To such as keep his covenant, and to those that remember his commandments to do them. The Lord hath prepared his throne in the heavens; and his kingdom ruleth over all. Bless the Lord, ye his angels, that excel in strength, that do his commandments, hearkening unto the voice of his word. Bless ye the Lord, all ye his hosts; ye ministers of his, that do his pleasure. Bless the Lord, all his works in all places of his dominion: bless the Lord, O my soul."

Retirement under GODS Pension Plan For man through the Holy Work of GOD-dependence is rewarding in and of itself. Certainly, GODS Might in our lives is displayed in plain view when we sincerely petition GOD in "Our Need and Dependence for GOD" to go before us in our every endeavor. Like the old school R&B song boasts "Don't Look Any Further" for it's all said, settled, and done in the Divinity of Holy scripture Psalm 103.

III. Seeking the Kingdom Of GOD

Exodus 7:1

"I have made you a GOD…"

For so many years of my life the only individuals I'd heard talking about the Goodness of GOD were preachers and those who were suffering victoriously over tribulation of some sort in some kind of seemingly miraculous way. What I failed to know about GOD they had come to know quite well. What they knew, I had forgotten. Oh, how easily we forget! We are "Created in the image and likeness of GOD" by GOD having dominion over all that GOD created. Realization of the "Spirit of GOD" power that GOD endowed and entrusted each of us with is Wisdom. It is the "Spirit of GOD Wisdom" GOD bestows on us that makes each of us a god to the pharaohs in our lives. Thus, we must first seek the Kingdom of GOD for it is our duty as Heirs to GOD's Goodness in the land of the living.

On August 8, 2008, GOD miraculously freed me from addiction to crack cocaine and cigarette smoking; GOD freed me on that very day! I had petitioned GOD day and night to please free me from my addictions. I'd become so tired of being a slave to mood-altering substances with the lascivious ignoble desires they conjured up in my body and mind. I was tired of always seeking but never finding nor having the Goodness of GOD visibly present in my life. However, that very day, a new lightweight, bright, clean sense of energy I'd never known settled over my body compelling sobriety. I'll never know why GOD Freed me from alcohol, cocaine, and cigarette addiction as others I know and personally got high with willfully perish in addiction. Nonetheless, I continue to walk in and with that spirit of GOD to this day and always. Seemingly, satanic forces present in my life were not happy with GOD gifting me freedom indeed with my sobriety.

On August 25, 2008, a city police officer pulled my car over stating it looked like my car was speeding to him. I was ordered from my car by the police officer and detained in the rear of his police car while he searched my vehicle. Upon returning to me handcuffed and locked in the back seat of his police car I was informed that my vehicle was being impounded. I was ticketed for speeding and released from custody of the police car's rear seat. Free to go my way. I walked away down the street. Suddenly I heard a noise as the police officer ran up to me screaming *"Stop, you're under arrest. You left this in my cruiser!!!"* In his hand was a plastic baggie with a white colored substance in it. I knew nothing about what this police officer was accusing me of doing. Clearly, I was literally being attacked by satanic tribulation!

On that day, August 25, 2008, spiritual warfare tribulation began anew in my life. I wasn't prepared in any way for this tribulation. I knew GOD was real, but I lacked trust in GOD's Ability and Willingness to protect me keeping me safe in every way in this strange tribulation. In my heart, mind, and soul I knew GOD did not create me, nor any human being, to be enslaved to satan through the sinful weakness of our flesh. I was suffering tribulation! I literally felt the forces of evil attacking me. So, I prayed, I praised, and I pleaded with GOD in every way I thought I knew how to free me from all my fears and wash me clean in His Righteousness. I had done nothing wrong.

Yet, I was accused of leaving drugs in a police cruiser. My denial of the police officer's accusation was ignored as if falling on deaf ears. The police officer arrested me, and transported me to the Ramsey County Adult Detention Center where I was held in custody for 72 hours and released pending further investigation; unbelievable. Throughout the 72 hours, I looked back over the years of my life stunned, realizing I could be innocently sent to prison. Man, Lord GOD JESUS CHRIST, help me, please! Shook to my core, I realized at that moment my addiction to crack cocaine, cigarettes, and alcohol had warped my understanding, perception, and appreciation of what GOD's Gift of Life to me, and all human beings, was predestined to be.

I had arrogantly taken control of what GOD had predestined for my life and focused on, leaning on, the satanic spirit of "I'm-ma-do self-dependence." Nonetheless, GOD Never gave up on me. It was GOD Alone Who freed me from the destructive clutches of cigarette smoking, crack cocaine addiction, and all desire for alcohol beverage consumption. Yet, for 20 years I chose, still have the right to choose, to honor the desires of my flesh rather than honor GOD's Real Deal. GOD's Real Deal is a primary job fully equipped with the very best pension plan in existence that leaves room with blessings for all else you put your hands to! Yes, now I know, being blind no more, GOD-dependence is my portion guaranteeing me victory in my every endeavor that is pleasing to GOD… *"Thine will be done on earth as it is in Heaven."* Then on October 7, 2008, I was notified by summons that I was charged with 5th Degree Possession of Crack Cocaine and ordered to appear for Arraignment at Ramsey County District Court.

How could this be happening? Lord GOD how can this be happening to me? Those words reverberated in my mind, in my head, repeatedly. I literally felt as though I was in a nightmare! There I stood miraculously free from bondage to cocaine, cigarettes, and alcoholic beverages only to be falsely accused of owning crack cocaine! So much bombarded my mind that seemed to be a prediction of doom. The facts presented to a jury would be my truthful denial pitted against the police officer's accusation. Oh, I was bewildered, and to my astonishment, I recalled reading Ezra 9:6:

"And I said: "O my God, I am too ashamed and humiliated to lift up my face to You, my God; for our iniquities have risen higher than our heads and our guilt has grown up to the heavens."

Yet, that very scripture in proper place and context turned out to be my portion temporarily. It's our way, the human way, to contemplate and entertain the justification of trauma in our lives by identifying the cause of it. I was shaken like never before trying to grasp why GOD was permitting this miscarriage of justice to happen to me. I had gotten by, but I hadn't got away! I reasoned that this was my payback for my sins.

Pressure bursts pipes: application of enough pressure mentally will send one's spirit into severe disquiet to the point of doing things against oneself. Not recognizing nor realizing that my "I'm-ma-do" need to be in control spirit was creating self-destructive scenarios in my mind. I considered asking my lawyer to petition the prosecution for a plea bargain with stayed imposition of any prison sentence. However, I just couldn't stomach the demeaning reality of entering a guilty plea to anything I did not do. My only legal and sane option was to have my lawyer file a petition with the court demanding DNA testing of the illegal item I was being accused of having possessed. DNA testing would certainly prove that I never possessed the illegal item the police officer accused me of leaving in his squad car. In my mind, a DNA test would free me of all accusations by the police. Finally, I had the tiger by its tail I arrogantly thought in my "I'm-ma-do" need to be in control spirit of self-dependence.

Now, GOD had miraculously freed me from the clutches of cigarettes, drugs, and alcohol yet, I now felt *"My"* rationale was ingeniously more legally equipped to deal with this satanic attack on my freedom than petitioning GOD Guide my lawyer in defending me. No, the lawyer was my servant, under my control, legally bound to honor my wishes in defending me at trial. Nonetheless, a rude awakening awaited me and my "I'm-ma-do spirit of self-dependence" at my jury trial.

Distraction from the realities of life is oftentimes a welcomed guest of our "I'm-ma-do" need to be in control spirit of self-dependence. Such was the case as I arrogantly demanded my lawyer file an appropriate brief petitioning the court to order a DNA Test Analysis of the Police Officer's alleged evidence for the presence of my DNA Profile. I knew I had done nothing wrong; I was being falsely accused by a police officer. Confident that DNA Analysis of the evidence would free me of the charge, I looked forward to my trial date and exoneration of the charge. I felt like I had been tried by evil forces and won! Nothing could go astray; nothing could defeat the lack of my DNA on the Police Officer's evidence against me. Truth can and will set us free – albeit when we obediently cry out for GOD's Guidance in total surrender of our "I'm-ma-do" spirit for jails sometimes become home to the innocent along with the guilty clearly realizing Romans 8:28;

"And we know that all things work together for good to those who love God, to those who are the called according to His purpose."

On March 9, 2009, my trial for 5th Degree Possession of Cocaine commenced. I hadn't seen my lawyer in over a month confident that DNA Analysis was going to set me free of the charge. However, when I got to the courtroom, I gave greetings to my lawyer and asked him for a status report on the DNA Analysis Testing for the presence of my DNA on the evidence I'd been accused of leaving in the squad car backseat. My lawyer stated that he failed to file a brief requesting court-ordered DNA Analysis Testing of the police evidence for the presence of my DNA Profile. A bomb went off filling my head with doom! I was flabbergasted! I couldn't contain myself; I interrupted court proceedings the first chance I had got. I immediately requested that the court indulge me in making court record of my lawyer's blatant disregard for my request for DNA Analysis Testing of the police evidence for the presence of my DNA Profile. The trial judge, Salvador Rosas, admonished me stating I was trying to avoid justice by attacking the "FINE ATTORNEY" the court had appointed me "flaunting your diamonds, gold, and fancy suit." At that very moment, I knew, I realized, that the Judge, Salvador Rosas, The Prosecuting Attorney, and my court-appointed Ramsey County Public Defender, Richard Sarette, were working together to boldly deprive me of my freedom by denying me due process of law – It worked for them. Three days later a Ramsey County Jury convicted me of 5th Degree Possession of Cocaine. The judge immediately ordered that I be taken into custody and held at Ramsey County LEC for sentencing. I was taken to jail, received my sentence a week later, and forgotten; I mean I was literally forgotten in this county jail or... being administered a type of additional jailhouse punishment. Nonetheless, after a month of waiting, I asked one of the fair-minded correctional officers why I had not been transported to prison like all other sentenced prisoners. It had been a month since I received a 21-month prison sentence with a mandate for chemical dependency treatment attached. After being laughed at, I was told I should've been transported to MCF-Saint Cloud weeks earlier. Finally, I was transported to MCF-Saint Cloud to begin my 21-month sentence.

My meeting with my prison case manager culminated with me being told I was mandated for treatment by the trial judge, but I had insufficient time left to serve to satisfy the court mandate for chemical dependency treatment completion. Therefore, any programming for me was out of reach due to the court-ordered treatment mandate taking prison programming priority. Here I was wrongfully convicted, a human parcel, being warehoused in time labeled useless to myself and worthless to the world. Locked away in bondage my determination to stay connected to, and grounded in, GOD'S Word and Promises was unwavering. GOD is all I had to sustain me, and I knew GOD would.

"But without faith it is impossible to please Him, for he who comes to God Must believe that He is, and that He is a rewarder of those who Diligently seek Him." (Hebrews 11:6-7)

GOD always has the last say in everything. Yes, my case manager staunchly asserted I would not be eligible for any prison programming due to my court-ordered treatment mandate, the long waiting line for prison programs, and my short prison term all working against me. My mind, my body, my soul, my spirit, yes, all of me knew none of those factors could deter me from applying for and acquiring the prison programming I wanted. Work release was what I wanted. GOD gave me exactly that! I was at peace with my circumstances. I didn't tell anyone about the letter I received by mail one day in November 2009 awarding me transfer to work release on February 10, 2010. As I was being taken for work release transfer on February 10, 2009, I was able to look my Prison Case Manager straight in the face as she arrived for work. My Supervised Release Date wasn't until July 3, 2010.

Upon arrival at work release, I readily found employment at a nonprofit manufacturing firm. Working Monday through Friday, 7:30 a.m. – 3:00 p.m., was ideal for my pending legal issues. My appeal was heard and granted by the Minnesota Court of Appeals, citing Defense Ineffective Assistance of Counsel, sending the conviction back to the Ramsey County trial court. However, the trial court set a January 19, 2011, hearing date for "Ineffective Assistance of Counsel" findings of the Minnesota Court of Appeals that overturned my conviction. Seemingly, out of judicial privileged meanness, the trial court scheduled the hearing for my overturned conviction for three months later. Yes, the trial court intentionally did all legally possible to keep me, unjustly convicted according to law, under the bondage of conviction for all but a mere two days before my overturned conviction would legally expire, releasing me from parole.

In October 2010, the Minnesota Court of Appeals overturned my 5th Degree Possession of Cocaine conviction citing Defense Ineffective Assistance of Counsel. On January 19, 2011, Trial Court Hearing on the Minnesota Court of Appeals Findings of Defense Ineffective Assistance of Counsel, Judge Rosas questioned my Attorney, Richard Sarette, as to why he had failed to file a motion for DNA testing of the States' Evidence for the presence of my DNA? Richard Sarette never uttered a word as he shrugged his shoulders turning his palms upwards finally muttering "I don't know." After admonishing Attorney Richard Sarette about the grave injustice, I, Johnnie R. Capers, suffered due to his ineffective assistance of counsel, Judge Rosas "Vacated" my 5th Degree Possession of Cocaine conviction. I later filed a petition with the court requesting compensation for my wrongful conviction, but the Ramsey County Prosecutor, John Choy, opposed my request stating that he felt that I was guilty as charged but for a legal technicality overturning my conviction by jury. In short, the Ramsey County Prosecutor viewed my constitutional right to DNA Test the States' Evidence as mere legal technicality unworthy of proving my innocence. The nightmare was far from over.

IV. Do You Remember 30 Years Ago?

"Enter by the narrow gate; for wide is the gate and broad is the way that leads to destruction..." (Matthew 7:13)

When I went to report to my parole officer in December 2010, she informed me that there was a detective from the Saint Paul Police Department in her office waiting to see me. I spoke with the detective and submitted to her; she took an inner jaw DNA Swab from me. The detective asked me questions about a homicide that occurred in the mid-90s in the city of Saint Paul, MN. I informed the detective I had no recollection of having ever encountered the murdered person. However, the detective stated that I was a person of interest linked by my DNA given in prison for the 5th Degree Possession of Cocaine conviction. The DNA swab taken from me in prison matched DNA found on clothing worn by the murder victim. I wasn't arrested and went my way that December day in 2010.

On December 11, 2019, Saint Paul Police pounded on my apartment door announcing, "SEARCH WARRANT, SEARCH WARRANT, OPEN UP NOW!!!" I immediately opened my front door to find police dressed in tactical gear with guns drawn pointing at me. I was immediately apprehended and advised that they had warrants to search my apartment and take me into custody. My fiancé was there with me witnessing all that occurred. Thus, having taken me into custody without incident, there was no need to search my apartment. I gave my permission for my fiancé to stay in my apartment while I was taken under arrest to jail for charge(s) unknown.

GOD'S Miracles Gracefully Favored me as in times before as I seemingly stood at disaster's door. Upon arrival at Saint Paul Police LEC, I was questioned once again about a woman who had been murdered and officially charged with 2 counts of 2nd Degree Murder for the woman's murder. I felt as if I'd been cast into hell under $150,000 bail. I felt so disastrously separated from GOD, locked away in a maze of hell jail whose walls whispered, *"We're your eternity…"* Oh, how I longed for, begged for, the word of GOD to soothe me in the hell my life choices had culminated in. I had advised my fiancé of what to do and she did exactly that. With the help of my fiancé's son-in-law, Greg, and my nephew-in-law, Martez, working with bail bondsman, Robert, my bail was posted as soon as the 72-hour judicial hold for formal charges expired.

I was in jail for 6 days before the Ramsey County Sherrif permitted me, allowed my, bail. Throughout the 6-day ordeal, GOD Carried me. The Word of GOD Kept me from losing my mind. Literally, it was GOD Alone Who saved my sanity. The acceptance of my bail took 6 days instead of the routine 3 days. At my request, I had spent the 6 days in solitary confinement refusing to chance any encounter with a "Lying Jailhouse Snitch" seeking a "Get Out of Jail Free Card" victim to invent lies about to sell to conviction hungry prosecutors. On day 2 of my 6-day jail stay, attorney friends of my nephew came to the jail to see me. I had spoken to these attorneys on the phone requesting them to please bring me a copy of Psalms 25, 27, and 119 when they come to speak with me about defending me against the two counts of 2nd Degree Murder. GOD Knows being able to read those Psalms to Him, to GOD, all alone in my requested solitary confinement jail cell gave me strength like that which GOD restored to Sampson. The Book of Psalms is medicine for my mind, body, and soul. I petition GOD to guide and protect me each day with words read from the Bible's Book of Psalms. My being able to read GOD'S Word soothes my soul just as my breathing GOD'S Breath of Life keeps my body alive.

Freedom has beauty that nothing can rival. After the sheriff electronically released me from jail that Monday morning of December 16, 2019, on $150,000 bail, the world of the 'footloose and fancy-free' was so sparkling brand new to me in every way. In my mind, my body, my soul, my spirit had been in the confines of hell for 6 days and 5 nights crying out to GOD in confession of every sin I could ever recall having committed. Oh, how I cried out to GOD for His forgiveness of my every sinful thought and desire committed in my wandering mind of carnal idleness. I knew that JESUS CHRIST Died Willfully for the sins of the world Granting Forgiveness of sin to all who come to JESUS CHRIST in Belief confessing their sins embracing agreement with GODS Word leading to Eternal Salvation and Blessings from GOD In JESUS CHRIST'S Holy Name. I remembered reading:

"That if you confess with your mouth the Lord Jesus and believe in your heart that God has raised Him from the dead, you will be saved. For with the heart one believes unto righteousness, and with the mouth, confession is made unto salvation. For the Scripture says, "Whoever believes on Him will not be put to shame." For there is no distinction between Jew and Greek, for the same Lord over all is rich to all who call upon Him. For whoever calls on the name of the Lord shall be saved." (Romans 10:9-13)

GOD Alone is, was, and will always be my salvation in every tribulation. For my belief is but a lie if I find reason for disagreement with GOD'S Word. As a sinner, I confess there is no justification for my sin that will ever stand before GOD. I had to embrace GOD'S Righteousness entirely without excuse nor second thought about GOD'S Ability and Willingness to save me from myself and those who seek to oppress and destroy me.

V.   Surviving the Trials and Tribulations

People want to know; there is no other way to describe their curiosity. The joyous, happy to see you, greetings often turned to outright inquisition. From December 16, 2019, until August 9, 2022, when my trial for 2cts of 2nd Degree Murder commenced, I endured the scrutiny of so many individuals who were convinced the presence of my DNA on the shirt worn by the victim was sufficient evidence for instant conviction as charged. Whispers, gossip, judgmental stares, even being outright called "Murderer" and "Rapist Murderer" a few times by individuals caused me to feel as though I'd been cut to the bone.

GOD Was, Is, Will Always Be my strength through the Saving Grace of JESUS CHRIST'S Holy Blood. I literally walked through hellfire for 6 days locked away in the county jail certain that only GOD could secure my $150,000 bail. I wrestled with demons of doubt in total isolation, unable to determine whether it was day or night, for the last 3 days of my 6-day stay. Seeking GOD with every fiber of my body I made up my mind to humbly surrender myself to GOD in complete trust by going forth in silence. I petitioned GOD in praise and prayer to guide my legal defense in every way. Upon my release on bail, I listened to, and entertained, advice from family and friends concerning hiring a lawyer. However, I just couldn't stomach; desperately looking to, looking for a person, a magical attorney, to save me if I had the right sum of money. In short, if I could produce the right sum of money the attorney would magically obtain my freedom. No, I put total trust in GOD to exonerate me of every charge, free of charge in GOD'S Righteousness. I felt it in my bones, I knew with every fiber of my body that only GOD Could and Would Save me from this seemingly certain destruction.

From December 16, 2019, through August 9, 2022, when my trial for 2cts of 2nd Degree Murder commenced I uttered not a word to assist my defense counsel. On one occasion, I merely asked my defense counsel to pray with me during my trial; That was three days into trial when my fiancé of 12 years abandoned me. I surmise much of the testimony was too unpleasantly gothic for her to stomach. Nonetheless, I doubled down on focusing on, trusting in, and knowing with every atom of my being that GOD Would vindicate me of every charge against me as Psalm 27 states:

1. *The Lord is my light and my salvation; Whom shall I fear? The Lord Is the strength of my life; Of whom all I be afraid?*
2. *When the wicked came against me To eat up my flesh, My enemies and foes, They stumbled and fell.*
3. *Though an army may encamp against me, My heart shall not fear; Though war may rise against me, In this I will be confident.*
4. *One thing I have desired of the Lord, That will I seek: That I may dwell in the house of the Lord All the days of my life, To behold the beauty of the Lord, And to inquire in His temple.*
5. *For in the time of trouble He shall hide me in His pavilion; In the secret place of His tabernacle He shall hide me; He shall set me high upon a rock.*
6. *And now my head shall be lifted up above my enemies all around me; Therefore I will offer sacrifices of joy in His tabernacle; I will sing, yes, I will sing praises to the Lord.*
7. *Hear, O Lord, when I cry with my voice! Have mercy also upon me, and answer me.*
8. *When You said, "Seek My face," My heart said to You, "Your face, Lord, I will seek."*
9. *Do not hide Your face from me; Do not turn Your servant away in anger; You have been my help; Do not leave me nor forsake me, O God of my salvation.*

10. *When my father and my mother forsake me, Then the Lord will take care of me.*
11. *Teach me Your way, O Lord, And lead me in a smooth path, because of my enemies.*
12. *Do not deliver me to the will of my adversaries; For false witnesses have risen against me, And such as breathe out violence.*
13. *I would have lost heart, unless I had believed That I would see the goodness of the Lord In the land of the living.*
14. *Wait on the Lord; Be of good courage, And He shall strengthen your heart; Wait, I say, on the Lord!* (Psalm 27)

My mind was made up and not to be changed. Often time, now abandoned by the woman I love, the days in court literally fighting for my life seemed to never end. I sat there in silence day after day feeling cut to the bone hemorrhaging the blood of love abandonment fighting off negative thoughts of doom with my Trust In GOD. The monstrous adjectives the prosecution was permitted to use in descriptive accusation against me were trying. Still, I could not permit anyone or anything to distract me from focusing on and trusting in GOD for my exoneration of every charge against me. So many times, as I sat there at the defense table with my attorneys, I gained strength to carry on in my recall of reading Biblical scripture that asserts those who wait on The LORD will be truly blessed suffering no shame. Thus, after all that could be said and done concluded, GOD, in JESUS CHRIST'S Holy Name was, is, will always be my saving salvation in all things.

On the afternoon of August 18, 2022, at 2:30 p.m., the jury reached their verdict. I was at home, with my niece Jessica, waiting when my attorney called with news of the verdict instructing me to get to the courtroom immediately. I felt so giddy, my knees almost buckled, as I got up from my couch to go to the Ramsey County Courthouse. Over and over, and over, again I kept speaking to GOD by reciting "The LORD'S Prayer" unceasingly. From the moment my ears heard my attorney say, "The jury has reached a verdict," on my cell phone, even unto the reading of the verdict, I recited "The LORDS Prayer" non-stop.

Finally, with all legal counsel assembled, the bailiff called the court to order. The judge then inquired of the jury foreperson as to whether the jury had reached a unanimous decision. The jury foreperson replied that the jury had indeed reached a unanimous verdict. The judge instructed the jury foreperson to read the jury's verdict to the court. The jury foreperson replied: "On Count 1, as contained in the indictment, we the jury find the defendant Not Guilty. On Count 2, as contained in the indictment, we the jury find the defendant Not Guilty." I went into a spirit-driven frenzy thanking and praising LORD GOD YAHWEH in JESUS CHRIST'S Holy Name for all in earshot to hear and possibly see! The judge admonished me by instructing my attorneys to control me. I listened to the judge, turned walked to the swinging spectator gate, and told my entourage of family and friends "Let us go from this place." With me leading the way, we exited the courtroom. Upon exiting the courthouse, still praising, thanking, and worshipping GOD I stooped down, got on my knees, and kissed the concrete walkway with cell phone cameras capturing the moment in time for eternity.

As Jessica drove me home from the Ramsey County Courthouse in downtown Saint Paul, Minnesota on that 18th day of August 2022, I felt like a little boy. I felt like the happy little boy I was who loved

Smokey Robinson's 1960's hit song "Hitch-Hike." I had to find my woman. Love holds no grudges, I was freed, free to be me, by the Hands of GOD be that good, bad, or indifferent in whosoever's mind. Truth speaks for itself; my mind was now focused on locating the woman I love; I had to know that she was all right in every way. I probably sound like a 1st rate fool to many of you reading this. However, I couldn't deny to myself the love I felt for that woman. In my mind, I fought off any thought that fostered feelings of being her fool with;

"Be not conformed to the world but transformed into likeness of JESUS CHRIST, GOD, Through GOD'S Word..." (Romans12:2)

I had to grant her, and myself, forgiveness for my perceived abandonment of me by her during my trial. I had to acknowledge that each of us is endowed by GOD with what GOD Designed to be fit for our individual personal assignment. GOD Never assigns any one of us more than we can handle. We must labor in GOD'S Love for the world helping each other to achieve GOD'S assignment for our individual lives securely knowing:

"No temptation has overtaken you except such as is common to man; But God is faithful, who will not allow you to be tempted beyond what you are able, but with the temptation will also make the way of escape, that you may be able to bear it." (1st Corinthians 10:13)

I no longer had the hammer of imprisonment hanging over my head. I was free, in good health with GOD'S Breath of Life in my lungs. A new feeling, a new meaning, in every way of GOD'S Renewing power of redemption energized my mind, body, and soul.

Praising GOD, I know that GOD alone has me still standing breathing HIS breath of life healthy, wealthy, wisely seeking daily transformation into image and likeness of JESUS CHRIST.

The days, weeks, months, over 2 years have gone by since that late August 2022 day when I called the woman I love to tell her my legal nightmare was over: Not Guilty by GOD'S Mighty hand! Yet, to this 20th day of May 2025, at 7:40 p.m. as I write these words our relationship endures the malnourishment of having common friends challenged by the dysfunctional turmoil of living daily exposed to acceptable drug addiction. Oh, what a cross we bear scuffling with alcohol, crack, opioid, sex, or any form of addiction. GOD Alone knows the seemingly never-ending personal nightmare addiction is to love, especially when love has evaded you for so long. For 20 years, from late November 1988 through August 8, 2008, I sought for, I searched for, I cried out for someone to love and love me back, albeit, seemingly helplessly, hopelessly enslaved to crack cocaine. From August 8, 2008, to August 18, 2022, I learned to navigate through the pain and endure the traumatic aftereffects of my 20-year crack cocaine addiction. Daily, I pick up my cross and bear it in love with hope of GOD enthusiasm for I know only GOD can deliver us from the evil satanic grasp of crack (now fentanyl laced) cocaine. GOD'S Will be done is the petition of my heart in Praise and Prayer thanking GOD unceasingly for HIS Grace and Mercy:

"How can you, being evil, speak good things? For out of the abundance of the heart the mouth speaks. A good man out of the good treasure of his heart brings forth good things, and an evil man out of the evil treasure brings forth evil things. But I say to you that for every idle word men may speak, they will give account of it in the day of judgment. For by your words

31

you will be justified, and by your words you will be condemned." (Matthew 12:34-37)

I will never forget, but it's so shameful to admit, the agonizing out-of-control despair I suffered every day of my addiction to crack cocaine. Being a prideful crack cocaine addict is costly, requiring the heart of a lion fueling the hellbent mind of a fool. Even now, right now, this very minute, my eyes fill with tears of sorrow and joy thanking LORD GOD for saving me from the literal "Living Hell" crack cocaine had made of my life. I thank GOD for the strength HE gives me to remain loving, faithful, and true to my woman of 15 years as I hold-on-tight, riding her rollercoaster of addiction. Some of you might wonder why I choose to remain in a relationship with a crack addict. So, I ask you to ponder this while examining your life:

"But if a wicked person turns away from all his sins that he has committed and keeps all my statutes and does what is just and right, he shall surely live; he shall not die .None of the transgressions that he has committed shall be remembered against him; for the righteousness that he has done he shall live. Have I any pleasure in the death of the wicked, declares the Lord God, and not rather that he should turn from his way and live?" (Ezekiel 18:21-23)

Above all else, disrespect of myself and of my woman by pursuing and wallowing in a carnal dead-end out of wedlock relationship with another woman has no appeal to me knowing such is repulsive to GOD alienating all involved in such wickedness from the Goodness of GOD. I must endure my woman's weaknesses in love painful though it be to me. I choose to wait on LORD GOD to heal our relationship according to His Will Being Done. I know GOD will direct me to move on if my woman enters a sexual relationship with someone else. Nonetheless, presently, the Grace, Love, Enduring Patience, and Forgiveness of GOD keeps me grounded waiting faithfully, lovingly, for GOD's Will to be done in our relationship. Being focused on GOD, quite plainly, made me realize there's lots of work for me to do in my relationship with GOD as GOD Works on the both of us. My woman and I, alike, are children of GOD journeying on earth according to GOD'S Master Plan. In love for GOD, I had to humbly embrace GOD'S Plan for her life with love as I focus unceasingly on GOD in praise, worship, prayer, and living testimony transformation into the image and likeness of JESUS CHRIST in my life. GODS Presence soothed me as I humbly longed for the company of my woman. Like a "Forest Gump" of sorts, my love, though pure and true, is of little consequence to the soul-stealing lure of crack cocaine, none whatsoever. Yet, no longer stuck in *"I'm-ma-do"* mode, I realize that the battle is LORD GODS in fulfillment of HIS Master Plan for our lives. So, I smile, genuinely smile, thanking GOD for now never forgetting all past, present, and promised future blessings lovingly depend on GOD'S eternal guidance.

On October 27, 2022, at approximately 3:30 a.m. GOD woke me to a feeling I'd never felt before. I struggled to sit up in bed feeling as though I was intoxicated. In darkness, sitting there on my bed, I leaned to my left side only to have my body just tip over. It was totally dark in my apartment. My left side wouldn't operate, it wouldn't perform its functions at all. Oh, LORD GOD, JESUS, JESUS, JESUS Please forgive me, please, please, please forgive me in JESUS CHRIST'S Holy Name! In total surrender to GOD in JESUS CHRIST'S Holy Name, I tearfully lay there in darkness reciting "The

Lord's Prayer" over and over awaiting my life end, awaiting death. I lay there praying The Lord's Prayer reminiscing my first encounter with GOD at the age of 9 when I woke up in bed, unable to move or speak, just see, breathe, and cry for GOD to save me for long periods of time. I've never forgotten my tearful peaceful surrender to GOD'S protection as I lay there helplessly in my bed on three occasions at the age of 9.

In prayerful surrender to GOD, in the darkness of my bedroom, I lay there for some minutes. Still filled with GOD'S Breath of Life, my soul's consciousness of the spirit of life still pulsating within my body filled me with need, human need, for my woman to swiftly come with her radiant love to my rescue. I managed to get my cell phone using the limbs of my right side. I called her, I called my woman but got no answer; feeling doomed, I called 911. Determined, feeling shame, calling out to GOD in JESUS CHRIST'S Holy Name, I was able to get to my front door to unlock it, as instructed, for the paramedics to gain entry to my apartment when they arrived. Stroke: the on-site diagnosis of my ailment was some type of stroke. A thankful sadness-filled joy overtook me knowing this cross shall I also victoriously bear in JESUS CHRIST'S Holy Name, Holy Blood, Holy Word. From past divine encounters, I knew quite well the heavenly joy yet to come from the cross-bearing pain in earthly over-coming spiritual bondage of sickness, mental illness, and addiction of every type. Wait on the LORD; Wait on LORD GOD!

GOD's Goodness
God's Pension Plan for Man

After the fall of Adam and Eve, GOD set Impossibility in the Simplicity of Obedience to HIS Laws, Commandments, and Every Word that proceeds out of the mouth of Lord GOD. The truth is JESUS CHRIST Alone is the only one that will ever be able to fulfill the Impossibility of obedience to GOD'S Laws and commandments. By obedience to GOD in all things, even unto death, for the sins of the world GOD Created for GOD to shower Love upon and be dependently loved back by Mankind reciprocally. JESUS CHRIST is the only Good One, the only Obedient One, the only one able to bear, to overcome, the desires of satanic carnality preying on all human flesh even unto suffering horrendous physical death, defying flesh in obedience to GOD'S Sinlessness. In the Garden of Eden, yet, even as Noah obediently entered the ark, GOD ordered him to build along with his family and all other living things GOD instructed to come; man's evilness continually increased. However, GOD never gave up on human beings as we continue to thrive to this very day in GOD'S Grace and Merciful Salvation JESUS CHRIST'S Holy Blood has Eternally granted us.

The reality of our creation and existence is to lovingly serve GOD in thoughts and deeds of praise, worship, and dependence on GOD to bless us, to prosper us, in our endeavors and works of our hands. Thus, Lord GOD makes it quite clear from times of old even to this day that provision attaches to all His assignments and promises:

"And I will make your descendants multiply as the stars of heaven; I will give to your descendants all these lands; and in your seed all the nations of the earth shall be blessed; because Abraham obeyed My voice and kept My charge, My commandments, My statutes, and My laws." (Genesis 26:4-5)

Always remember, whether Christian, Islamic, Jew or believe in GOD as a Higher Power, please never ever forget that GOD counting Abraham's belief as righteousness continues today and for eternity, just as in times of Genesis 15:6; *"And he believed in the Lord; and he counted it to him for righteousness."*

Our belief in the saving blood of Lord GOD, JESUS CHRIST, is counted as righteousness that washes away GOD'S remembrance of our every sin, opening the Holy Gates of eternal life for all who believe. Now, recalling that GOD always attaches provision to all His promises starting in the book of Genesis evidenced by, and in the text of Genesis 26:13-14:

"The man began to prosper, and continued prospering until he became very prosperous; for he had possessions of flocks and possessions of herds and a great number of servants. So the Philistines envied him."

Children of GOD have endured the disdain of envious worldly people throughout world history to this very day due to their GOD Given Provision of Goodness in the land of the living:

"Say to the righteous that it shall be well with them, For they shall eat the fruit of their doings. Woe to the wicked! It shall be ill with him, For the reward of his hands shall be given him." (Isaiah 3:10–11)

We must take note that the righteous eat the fruit of their doings while the wicked are given the reward of his hands. The righteousness GOD attributes to man is divinely attached to man's Dependence on GOD, trusting GOD totally, in all things as stated by JESUS CHRIST in The Lord's Prayer: *"Thine kingdom come. Thine will be done on earth as it is in Heaven."* (Matthew 6:10). King David, whom GOD classified as *"The Lord has sought for Himself a man after His own heart,"* (1 Samuel 13:14), further reveals the divine provisions GOD reserves for all who focus unceasingly on GOD in the morning, late at night, and all through the day:

"Blessed is the man who walks not in the counsel of the [a]ungodly, Nor stands in the path of sinners, nor sits in the seat of the scornful; but his delight is in the law of the Lord, And in His law he meditates day and night. He shall be like a tree Planted By the rivers of water, that brings forth its fruit in its season, whose leaf also shall not wither; And whatever he does shall prosper. The ungodly are not so, but are like the chaff which the wind drives away. Therefore, the ungodly shall not stand in the judgment, Nor sinners in of the righteous. For the Lord knows the way of the righteous But the way of the ungodly shall perish." (Psalm 1)

Thus, from my Holy Scripture knowledge and the many marvelous miracles GOD has performed in my life, it became evident, so noticeably clear to me, that GOD has a pension plan for man that surpasses the most lucrative Fortune 500 Company pension plan known to man. Despite all the trials, tribulations, ugly financial setbacks, and devasting disappointments yearning true love in my life, GOD alone has kept me healthy, wealthy, and wise radiantly smiling blessing and favor upon me unceasingly. I know firsthand from knowledge revealed to, experienced by, me personally that those who wait on LORD GOD want for no good thing.

I was 13 years old when I declared my independence from beatings with extension cords, braided tree-switch whippings, face slaps, and daily verbal berating and curses, predicting I wouldn't make it to age 21. Honestly, there was one choice festering in my wayward mind; I must leave home and make it on my own. Off and on, I've spent at least 12 years of my life confined in jails and prisons that might have been better spent earning my PhD. It is a miracle that I of sound mind, body, and spirit can compose this book for you. According to the rule of this natural, physical world I should be penniless, totally without any good thing, in poor health at the mercy of the world. GOD'S Grace, Mercy, and Favor declare just the opposite. GOD'S promise to, covenant with, Abram extends to Abraham's descendants to this day:

"After these things the word of the Lord came to Abram in a vision, saying, "Do not be afraid, Abram. I am your shield, your exceedingly great reward." (Genesis 15:1)

Therefore, GOD makes it clear to His children that having overcome the world through transformation into the image and likeness of JESUS CHRIST provision from GOD beyond your wildest imagination is your portion. In short; "The Deal is Real: GODS Pension Plan for Man, exists eternally. The word of GOD Demands all things to work together for the good of all who love LORD God. Be not deceived, nor deceive yourself, for "LOVE Is GOD." Talk of loving GOD is convicting of the soul, for our flesh is weak. Still, in weakness, Love manifests itself in actions born of thoughts navigating to what is loved, played out in deeds expressing GOD Is Love replete in JESUS CHRIST'S Words, *"If you love me, keep My commandments,"* (John 14:15). The Deal Is Real: GODS Pension Plan For Man, is Spiritual Security over Social Security, with GOD Funded 401K Plan, and GODS Hands Health Care Universal. Apply now by your thoughts, words, and deeds. "The Deal Is Real: GODS Pension Plan For Man.

Epilog

Each of us was born into the world as a GOD Created Gift of Love that is dependent on, defenseless to, and innocent of being human Created in the Image and Likeness of GOD. From the black topsoil of the earth, GOD formed the first man and breathed GOD'S Breath of life into the man's nostrils naming him "Adam." The "Man" Adam, and the "Woman," Eve, made from a rib taken out of Adam's side by GOD are living souls called Mankind, Human Beings, that GOD Created. Mankind was, is, and will always be GOD'S most loved and prized creation. Adam and Eve were created to live forever with GOD Given Provision for their every need, want, and desire as stewards over all GOD created while rendering unceasing worship-filled praise and prayer to GOD as their primary job.

"For we are God's fellow workers; you are God's field, you are God's building. According to the grace of God, which was given to me, as a wise master builder, I have laid the foundation, and another builds on it. But let each one take heed how he builds on it. For no other foundation can anyone lay than that which is laid, which is JESUS CHRIST." (1 Corinthians 3:9-11)

Thus, have we forsaken and forgotten our "Job of Holy Honor" replete with "GODS Pension Plan for Man" established by GOD in the Garden of Eden? Have we lost sight of why man, unlike all other creation, was intricately formed by the loving hands of GOD into the Image and Likeness of GOD with GOD'S Breath of Life still being breathed into the nostrils of all mankind (to this very day) forming life's first word sound *"Yahweh"* at life's *1st breath in-YAH* and *1st breath out-WEH* joined together as one as are *The Father, GOD, and The Son, JESUS CHRIST,* for man's wellbeing in this land of the living that is besieged by soul stealing satanic wiles, illusions, and influences?

Oh, how wonderfully beautiful life appears in the vigor of youth laboring to successfully conform to the world's carnal values in the blindness of self-dependence. Born of Satan, the idolatrous *"I'm-ma-do Spirit"* of self-dependence alienates us from GOD'S Preordained Blessings for us. We spend years of our lives, THE YOUNGER YEARS OF OUR LIVES, stuck on *"I'm-ma-do"* self-dependence doing acrobatics of conformity to the values of the societal environments we dwell in. *"I'm-ma show you what "I'm-ma-do!" Baby, it's me, we, us, against the world!"* affirmations sound good and self-empowering, guiding one's mind, soul, and spirit away from any daily need of giving Glory, Praise, and Honor to GOD, but promote satanic strongholds of self-dependence to take residence in one's being. As age visits one's body, the Holy Spirit of GOD knocks seeking loving 'Welcome Home' residence in one's mind, body, and soul for spiritual redemption by the Saving Blood of JESUS CHRIST. However, not everyone recovers gracefully from the satanic idolatrous *"I'm-ma-do"* spirit of self-dependence spiritually alienated from belief, faith, and trust in GOD via JESUS CHRIST.

"Delight yourself also in the Lord, And He shall give you the desires of your heart. Commit your way to the Lord, Trust also in Him, And He shall bring it to pass. He shall bring forth your righteousness as the light, And your justice as the noonday." (Psalm 37:4-5)

The righteousness GOD attributed to Abraham by which GOD declared all families of the earth would be blessed is replete with provision. Abraham wanted not for GOD-accounted righteousness to Abraham's belief in every word that proceeded from the mouth of LORD GOD. Therefore, shame nor lack are GOD'S predestined portion for any Child of GOD for GOD Will provide, even miraculously, for His Children marveling the minds of many in this present day and age of proud self-righteous self-dependence.

GOD'S Pension Plan for Man is joyfully spoken of by King David in the words of Psalm 1 as if a handwritten job description directing the way to and enjoyment of GOD'S righteousness while foretelling the imminent end of the ungodly:

"Blessed is the man who walks not in the counsel of the ungodly, nor stands in the path of sinners, nor sits in the seat of the scornful; But his delight is in the law of the Lord, and in His law he meditates day and night. He shall be like a tree planted by the rivers of water, that brings forth its fruit in its season, whose leaf also shall not wither; and whatever he does shall prosper. The ungodly are not so, but are like the chaff which the wind drives away. Therefore, the ungodly shall not stand in the judgment, nor sinners in the congregation of the righteous. For the Lord knows the way of the righteous, but the way of the ungodly shall perish." (Psalm 1 NKJV)

The reality that separates so many of us from taking claim of the Holy Inheritance GOD bequeathed to all Human Beings by Divine Heavenly Ordinance is a lack of understanding the "Satan Controlling" power in grasping and utilizing this reality:

"For if by the one man's offense death reigned through the one, much more those who receive abundance of grace and of the gift of righteousness

will reign in life through the One, JESUS CHRIST. Therefore, as through one man's offense judgment came to all men, resulting in condemnation, even so through one Man's righteous act the free gift came to all men, resulting in justification of life. For as by one man's disobedience many were made sinners, so also, by one Man's obedience, many will be made righteous. Moreover, the law entered that the offense might abound. But where sin abounded, grace abounded much more, [21] *so that as sin reigned in death, even so grace might reign through righteousness to eternal life through JESUS CHRIST our Lord."* (Romans 5:17-21)

www.ingramcontent.com/pod-product-compliance
Lightning Source LLC
Chambersburg PA
CBHW051248120626
46547CB00014B/1842